My cake was on display in the fam

1

"Come on, everyone," my father called. "It's nearly time for Pete to make a wish. Then we can all have cake."

"Good!" said my mother.

"Great!" said my brother Sam. "I've been waiting for this cake all day."

"I think we're all here," said my grandmother.

"Close your eyes, Pete," said Dad.

"Make a wish, then blow."

I was all set to make my wish.

Then my mother said, "Wait a second!

I left the light on in the other room.

I'll be right back."

She went to the other room to turn out the light.

My mother returned.

Once again, everyone was there.

"All set, Pete?" my father asked.

"All set," I said.

Then Sam said, "Wait a second! I want to get the cat. I think Tiger should be here, too."

So Sam went to look for the cat.

8

Sam returned with Tiger.

Once again, everyone was there.

"All set, Pete?" my mother asked.

"All set," I said.

Then my grandmother said, "Wait a second!

I smell smoke. I'd better go see about the bread.

I'll be right back."

My grandmother ran out of the room.

My grandmother returned with the bread.
Once again, everyone was there.
She looked unhappy, but the rest of us started
to laugh. Her white bread was very brown!
"I left the bread in too long," said my
grandmother sadly.
"We like it like that!" we all said.

"Well," asked my mother, "should we try again?"

"I'm all set," I said.

Then my father said, "Wait a second!
I want to take a picture while we're all together.
I'll be right back." Then he left the room.

My father came back.

Once again, everyone was there.

"All set, Pete?" asked my grandmother.

"All set," I said.

But then I looked down at the cake.

"There isn't anything left to blow out!" I said.

"But you can still make a wish,"
said my grandmother.

I said, "I wish you all would just STAY here,
so we can have some cake!"

Everyone laughed.

Then, at last, we had our cake.

We were about to eat it, when my father said,

"Wait a second!" and he took our picture!